SO YOU WANT TO GROW A TACO?

BY BRIDGET HEOS • ILLUSTRATED BY DANIELE FABBRI

AMICUS ILLUSTRATED • AMICUS INK

Amicus Illustrated and Amicus Ink
are imprints of Amicus
P.O. Box 1329
Mankato, MN 56002

Library of Congress Cataloging-in-Publication Data
Heos, Bridget, author.
 So you want to grow a taco? / by Bridget Heos ; illustrated by Daniele Fabbri.
    pages cm. — (Grow your food)
 Summary: "A young boy wants to grow his own tacos, learns where the many ingredients come from, and learns how to grow corn and make tortillas. Includes kid-friendly taco recipe"—Provided by publisher.
 ISBN 978-1-60753-742-7 (library binding)
 ISBN 978-1-60753-909-4 (ebook)
 ISBN 978-1-68152-015-5 (paperback)
1. Corn—Juvenile literature. 2. Tacos—Juvenile literature. 3. Tortillas—Juvenile literature. 4. Gardening—Juvenile literature. I. Fabbri, Daniele, 1978- illustrator. II. Title. III. Series: Heos, Bridget. Grow your food.
 SB191.M2H49 2016
 633.1'5—dc23   2014041496

Editor: Rebecca Glaser
Designer: Kathleen Petelinsek

Printed in the United States of America at Corporate Graphics in North Mankato, Minnesota.

HC 10 9 8 7 6 5 4 3 2 1
PB 10 9 8 7 6 5 4 3 2 1

ABOUT THE AUTHOR

Bridget Heos is the author of more than 70 books for children including *Mustache Baby* and *Mustache Baby Meets His Match*. She has had a garden since fifth grade and is currently growing tomato sauce and pumpkin and cherry pie. You can find out more about her at www.authorbridgetheos.com.

ABOUT THE ILLUSTRATOR

Daniele Fabbri was born in Ravenna, Italy, in 1978. He graduated from Istituto Europeo di Design in Milan, Italy, and started his career as a cartoon animator, storyboarder, and background designer for animated series. He has worked as a freelance illustrator since 2003, collaborating with international publishers and advertising agencies.

Tacos are terrific. But have you ever wondered where they come from? Like all food, they come from plants and animals. You could even grow a taco at home.

There's no such thing as a taco plant, of course.

But you can grow the ingredients.

For the tortillas, you'll need corn. For the meat, you'll need beef cows. The cheese will come from dairy cows.

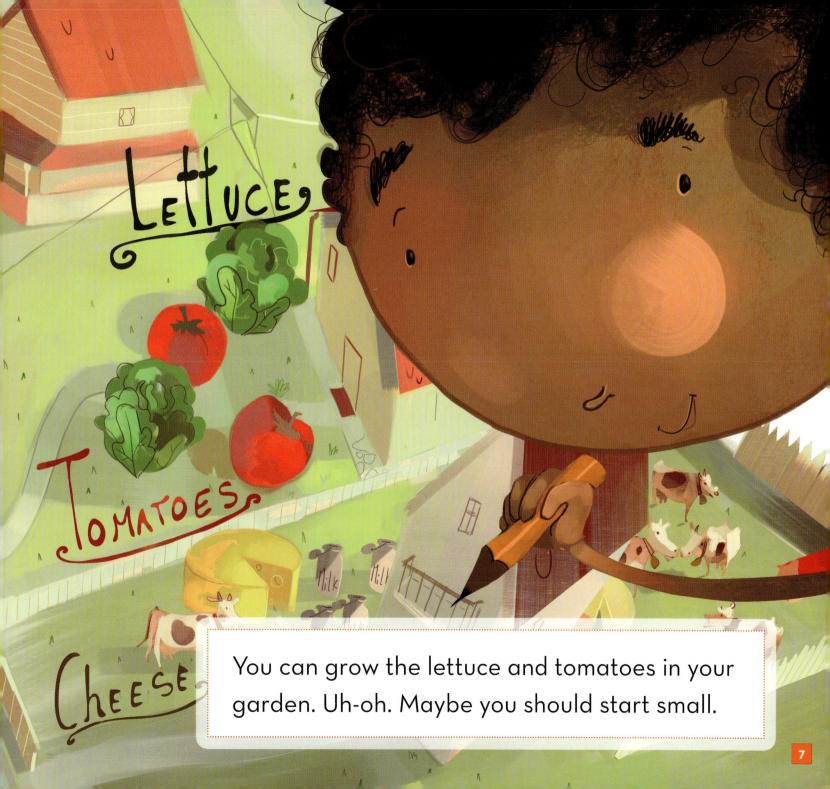

You can grow the lettuce and tomatoes in your garden. Uh-oh. Maybe you should start small.

Let's say you want to make the corn tortillas. First you have to plant the corn. Did you know that the kernels that you eat are also the seeds planted to grow corn?

And you'll need to take care of the seeds. Think of it this way: We eat corn, but corn needs to eat, too! Corn food is sunlight, water, and the nutrients found in soil.

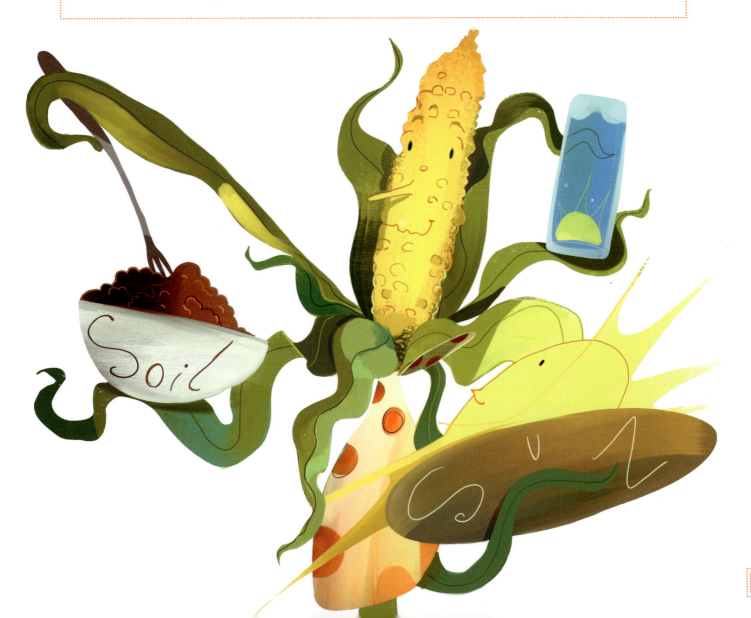

Find a sunny spot in your yard.

10

Line your garden with stones or a wooden frame. Then add the soil.

Corn likes the soil to be really warm. Different parts of the country get warm at different times. Check the seed packet for the best time to plant where you live.

When you plant, remember that corn grows big and tall. And it doesn't like being crowded.

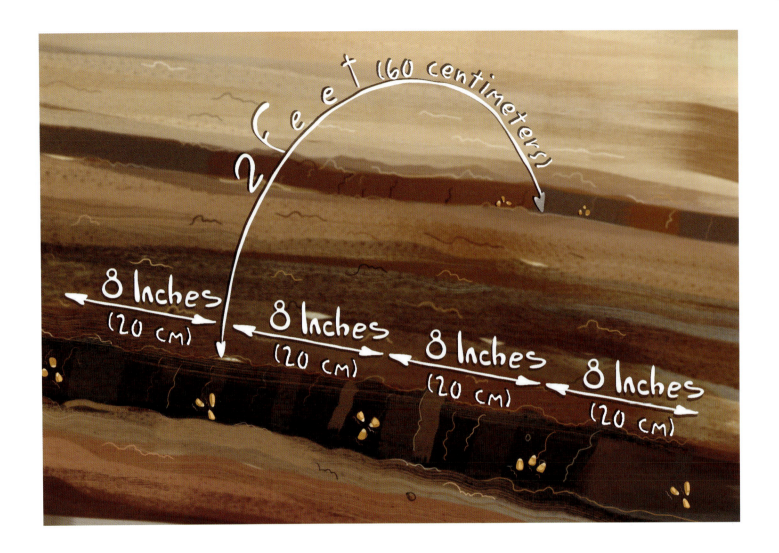

So leave plenty of space between rows. In each row, sow a few seeds into a small hole. Leave some space, and then plant a few more. Keep going along the row.

Water your seeds . . . and wait for them to grow. But you won't have to wait that long! Corn grows fast! Some people say that corn grows so fast that you can almost hear it grow.

To make tortillas, you need to let the ears dry on the stalk. Then harvest the corn, and hang it up to dry some more. Twist the dry corn so that it falls off the cob.

Then have a grown-up help you make the tortillas. There are a lot of steps!

Step 1: Boil the corn.

Step 2: Soak the corn.

Step 3: Grind the corn.

Step 4: Press the corn mush into a flat tortilla.

Step 5: Cook the tortilla.

Now it's taco time! Uh-oh! The tortillas are empty. What are you going to put in your tacos?

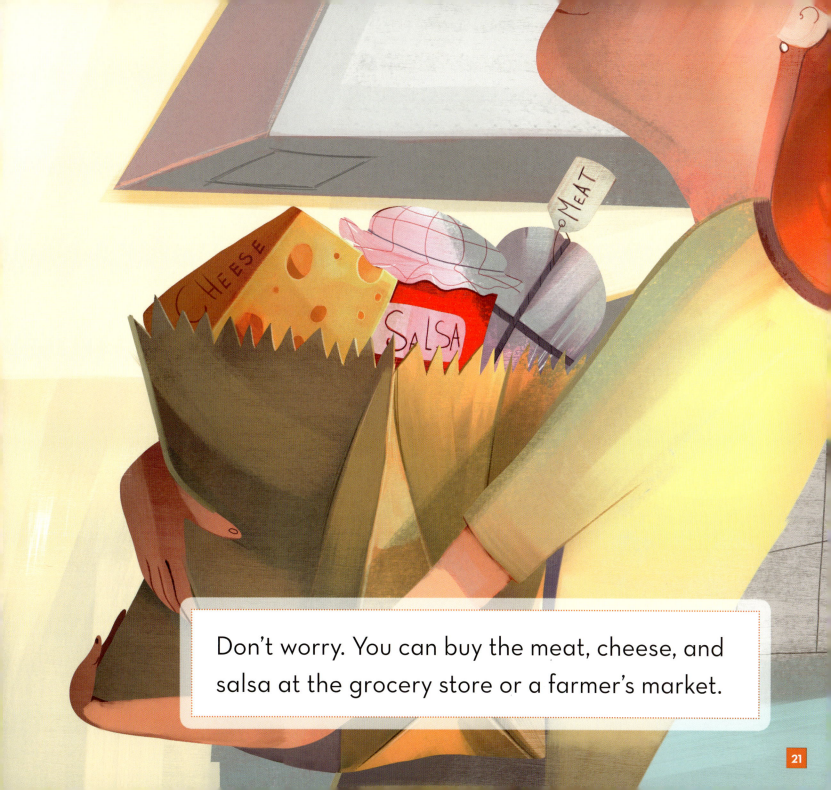

Don't worry. You can buy the meat, cheese, and salsa at the grocery store or a farmer's market.

And next year, you can add some of the taco toppings to your garden!

MAKE YOUR OWN TACO BAR

INGREDIENTS

- tortillas
- thinly sliced beef or chicken
- black beans
- tomato
- red onion
- cilantro
- avocado
- lime
- cheese
- sour cream

WHAT YOU DO

1. Drain and rinse the black beans. Place them in a bowl with a little salt.
2. Ask an adult to help you cook the meat and then put it in a bowl.
3. Chop the tomato, red onion, and cilantro. Add salt to taste. Toss them together in a bowl.
4. Peel and slice the avocado. Put it in a bowl.
5. Cut the lime into quarters. Place these in a bowl.
6. Shred your favorite cheese into a bowl.
7. Give everyone a couple of your homemade tortillas and let them make their own tacos!

GLOSSARY

cob The part of corn on which kernels grow.

ear The part of corn that includes the cob and the husks.

harvest To pick vegetables, fruit, or other plants that are ready to be used.

sow To plant seeds.

stalk The primary stem of a plant.

READ MORE

Kuskowski, Alex. **Super Simple Salad Gardens: A Kid's Guide to Gardening**. Minneapolis: ABDO Publishing Co., 2015.

Murray, Laura. **Corn**. Mankato, Minn.: Creative Education, 2015.

Nelson, Robin. **From Kernel to Corn**. Minneapolis: Lerner, 2012.

WEBSITES

The Great Corn Adventure
urbanext.illinois.edu/corn
Learn about the history of corn and how it is farmed today through a narrated slideshow.

KidsGardening: Helping Young Minds Grow
www.kidsgardening.org
The National Gardening Association has tips on how to start a garden at home or at school.

My First Garden: A Children's Guide
urbanext.illinois.edu/firstgarden
Learn about the world of fun and clever gardening with step-by-step information on how to start a garden.

Every effort has been made to ensure that these websites are appropriate for children. However, because of the nature of the Internet, it is impossible to guarantee that these sites will remain active indefinitely or that their contents will not be altered.